DINING ETIQUETTE

DINING ETIQUETTE

Essential Guide for Table Manners, Business Meals, Sushi, Wine and Tea Etiquette

By Rebecca Black

CELESTIAL ARC PUBLISHING

Revised 2019

CELESTIAL ARC PUBLISHING

ISBN-13: 978-1500221942
ISBN-10: 1500221945

DEDICATION

To my dearest friend and loving husband Walker Black. You have been my most ardent supporter and the very best editor a writer can have.

CONTENTS

INTRODUCTION

Why write another etiquette book on table manners? Surprisingly, I found that there are few resources for finding credible answers to your table manners questions. Thus, I wanted to bring my twenty-plus years of etiquette consulting experience to your table.

Our world is shrinking, exposing us to various previously unknown table manners styles. This is especially true when we discover a special food we want to enjoy in the most traditional way, such as sushi. Accordingly, it becomes important to know these various table manners styles.

Table manners is also vitally important for business meals, as everything we do during these sessions is scrutinized—especially when the interview is over a meal.

Wine Etiquette and *How to Tea* is also included in this book. Why? I've found that the love of wine is spreading on such a large scale, that most of California is littered with vineyards. Similarly, I've noted the resurgence in popularity of teahouses, tea parties, and just plain tea. As an etiquette consultant, I receive at least one tea-party etiquette session per month. It is just that popular.

These topics tend to be most popular. However, if you find that your questions are not answered, please contact us for answers.

CHAPTER ONE

TABLE MANNERS—THE BASICS

THE IMPORTANCE OF TABLE MANNERS

"Animals feed, men eat, but only wise men know the art of dining" French Gastronome. *Anthelme Brillat-Savarin*

Why is it that we think of table manners when someone mentions etiquette? Perhaps it is because we use most of our manners at the table.

What worries you about your table manners skills? Most likely, you are worried about picking up the wrong fork at a formal meal. Not to worry, none of us uses five forks at a meal anymore, and why should we. Our tables are rarely set with a full set of flatware and to be honest, the most important rule for the table is this: Everyone should feel comfortable at the table, so we avoid behaviors that would make our tablemates uncomfortable.

So, do we throw all ideas of table manners out with the dishwater? Absolutely not. We still need guidelines.

Before we begin, though, it is best to learn a bit of history and trivia, so we have a good appreciation of what table manners are and how it has evolved.

A BIT OF HISTORY

History tells us that the first modern eating utensil was the knife. During early Roman times, we all carried our eating utensil with us; these were used more as a stabbing and slicing utensil and were even buried with us.

As time marched on, knives remained a popular eating utensil. We even find that knives were used at the table in 5th century, Saxon England. It appeared that men always carried one for their own use and to cut meat for women.

How about the rounded edge knife? In France, many years ago, 1669 to be exact, there was a King Louis. This King, King Louis XIV, decided that to have weapons at the table was not a great idea. Therefore, he created a law stating that all table knives were to be rounded. This is the reason that in present times, we place our knives with the rounded edge pointing inward toward our plate when we set the table. We don't point our *weapon* toward anyone.

How about the first fork? The fork came from the area now known as Turkey, although some think that it may have originated from Greece. It was big and beautiful, much too expensive for most people to use and it wasn't very useful. It was too large and had only two prongs—food slipped through.

Therefore, for many years, only the rich and famous of the day used it. It took many years for the fork to travel to people who would use it, besides royalty.

In the 1500s, the Italians made the fork useful for the masses and they used it for many years before Catherine de Médicis took it to France when she married Henry II.

In the 1600's an explorer presented the fork to the people of England. The English thought of it as something a feeble-minded person would use, because why would anyone use something like that when God gave us ten fingers?

SETTING THE TABLE

An informal place setting would have a salad fork on the far left of the plate (Americans usually eat salad for a first course) with the dinner fork next to it, closest to the plate. The napkin is placed to the left of the forks or in the center of the plate, if the dinner is formal. The plate is in the center of the place setting. If soup is on the menu, the bowl is usually placed on top of the plate. The knife and spoon(s) are placed on the right of the plate with the sharp edge of the knife pointed toward the plate.

Glasses are placed above the knife in descending order per size. Many people enjoy wine with dinner; if this is the case, there is a water glass above the knife and a wine glass, or two, to its right.

If a bread plate is used, it is placed above the forks with the spreader across the top of the plate, rounded side of the knife pointed toward you.

If a bread plate is used, it would be placed above the forks with the spreader across the top of the plate, rounded side of the knife pointed toward you.

While we could discuss formal place settings here, it is not necessary. Utensil placement and number is logical. With each course, you would use a different utensil; for example, if you will be serving a salad, a fish course and an entrée you would set three forks to the left of the plate to be used in the order in which you eat the courses.

TABLE BEHAVIOR

 Basic manners are essential in everything we do and a definite must at the table. The basic and most important rule of the table is that we always want everyone to feel comfortable, because the essence of good manners is caring for those around you. If we keep this in mind, more than likely we will make the right decision. So, we would always use all our manners like please, thank you, excuse me and please pass the… And, when someone asks for the salt, pass the pepper also. These two, travel in pairs.

USE THE UTENSIL THAT MAKES THE MOST SENSE

An easy rule to follow is to use the utensil that makes the most sense. Say that you are faced with a dish which includes chunky food in a yummy sauce. You may want to use a fork because you want to stab the chunks of food items. However, if you want to taste the sauce, you may want to use your spoon. This is a personal decision and both choices are correct. Just choose the utensil that makes the most sense for you to use at that time.

If the following course requires the utensil you just used and it has been removed, no problem. For this type of meal, you could simply ask for another utensil or it will be brought out for you automatically.

WAIT UNTIL ALL ARE SERVED

Additionally, wait until all are served to begin eating. If we begin to eat before everyone is served, we appear greedy. This rule derives from a very old rule in which we would wait for the hostess to pick up her fork. This is tantamount to the dinner bell ringing.

ABOUT YOUR NAPKIN

Women, please try to avoid leaving lipstick marks on your glass by blotting your lips before the meal begins. Use a tissue, not your napkin. Speaking of napkin use, use your napkin to blot your mouth before drinking, as food and grease marks on the rim of a glass are unsightly.

If your napkin is a flimsy paper napkin, it isn't necessary to place it on your lap as you may get food on your clothes. When using one, you may place it on the table after blotting your mouth. Just try to conceal any food bits, so you don't make the other diners uncomfortable. Perhaps you could also place a clean napkin in your lap that will not be used to protect your clothes from spills.

NAPKIN RULES

Placed the napkin on the left of the place setting or on the plate if the dinner is formal and in your lap after everyone has been seated. If you leave the table for a moment, place the napkin to the left of the plate or on the chair. Blot your mouth before taking a drink. Neatly place the napkin to the right of the plate when finished.

STRANGE FOODS

There are many types of food for which we may not be acquainted. In fact, in the United States, we didn't receive our first kiwi until the eighties. It seems as if we are faced with new foods every day now. So, if you are ever in doubt of what to do with a food or utensil during a meal, watch what the host does.

OBSCURE RULES

This may be an obscure rule, but we should cut and eat only one bite at a time. When we cut more than a few bites of food at one time it appears as if we are overly eager to finish the meal. And, we wouldn't want those around us to feel as if we are anxious to leave the table.

Another obscure, slightly used rule these days is that children should wait until the adults are seated before sitting. This is a very old-fashioned rule that many do not observe. However, it may be observed during formal meals. Hence, be aware.

Do not blow on hot food. It seems as if everyone does this. So, why is this behavior incorrect? It is logical if you think about it. If you blow on your food, you could share more than conversation by accidentally blowing bits of food on other diners and sharing germs. You may also seem overly interested in speeding up your meal.

SENSITIVE ISSUES

Sometimes we can have something in our mouths that is very unpleasant such as gristle or a bone. The protocol for removing this unpleasantness from the mouth is to spit it out discretely onto the same utensil used to put it in our mouth and place it on our plate. Please try to be as discreet as possible.

There is no way to be discreet when we need to sneeze or cough. When the urge strikes, we sneeze and cough into our napkin pointing our head away from the table and follow it with, "Excuse me." However, if we must blow our nose or if we are coughing extensively, we excuse ourselves from the table—we never blow our nose into our napkin. This is simply displaying respect for others at the table.

ELBOWS IN!

A great oldie but goodie rule is the one about our elbows. We all know this one: elbows should be close to our sides, not flapping about or placed on the table. However, did you know that we may place our elbows on the table in certain circumstances? Absolutely! The one exception is when you are having a conversation with a tablemate. If you place your utensils down on the plate, you may lean forward with an elbow on the table. This body language conveys that you are interested in what he or she is saying.

MOTHER RECOMMENDED RULES

Do you remember your mother telling you to chew with your mouth closed? Watching someone eat with his mouth open is disgusting. No one wants to view your half-eaten food as you slosh it around in your mouth. Therefore, we should chew with our mouths closed.

Another excellent *mother recommendation* is to take one bite at a time never overstuffing your mouth. If your face is distorted, you have too much in your mouth; and please, chew without talking. Food flying everywhere is nauseating.

BREAD AND BUTTER RULES

Finally, if using butter with bread, follow these steps. Using the butter knife, take a portion of butter and place it on your bread plate. Tear one piece of the bread or roll; spread the butter on the bread with your butter spreader, then take a bite.

- Your bread plate is on your left above your forks.

- Take one piece of bread at a time.

- Put butter on your plate with the butter knife or place knife.

- Tear one piece of bread and butter that piece.

- Eat one piece of bread at a time.

As important as it is to know what we *should* do at the table, we need to know what we should *not* do. Here are some absolute do not (s).

DO NOT

- Hover over your food.

- Hold your utensils like shovels.

- Reach.

- Place a utensil on the table after it is used.

- Blow on hot food.

- Wear any type of hat at the table.

- Make rude noises or engage in bad habits at the table.

- Lick your fingers.

- Push food onto your fork using your fingers.

Always remember that all manners derive from the basic instinct to treat people kindly. So, it follows, that we would want everyone at the table to feel comfortable.

CHAPTER TWO

HOLDING & USING UTENSILS

HOW TO BEGIN

Now that the table is set, it is time to be seated. Place napkins in laps after everyone is seated at the table. There are a few reasons for this. One reason is that it is customary for men to rise as ladies enter the dining room. Another is that you would not want to appear to be overly anxious to get to the meal. After all, people are more important than the food.

With everyone seated at the table, napkins in laps and food on the plates, it is time to discuss proper utensil use. There are two methods of using our utensils. One is the Continental method, which is used in Europe (most people who use fork, knife and spoon use this method) and the other is our zigzag or American method. One has to wonder why there are two different methods. Well, here too there are two theories about how this came about.

THE AMERICAN METHOD

AMERICAN METHOD TRIVIA

The first theory about how the American Method began is boring but probably true. In the 1600s, we Americans were cut off from Europe by distance and culture. There was one account of a Governor Winthrop of the Massachusetts Bay Colony using a fork in our colonial America. The rest of us, however, had no forks because they were too expensive, so we continued to use the blunted knives imported from Europe.

Because these were not easy to eat with, we began to use our spoon to steady food while cutting. We would then have to switch the spoon to the right hand to scoop up the bite of food.

The second, sexier (yes, table manners can be sexy), theory draws us to the times leading up to the American Revolution. The theory postulates that because one could never know who was on which side of the conflict, the revolutionists devised a method of identifying each other. They would enter a pub or eating establishment and the person who placed his knife down and switched hands to eat their bite was a fellow revolutionary.

It really doesn't matter which theory is correct, but the second is much more exciting.

HOW TO USE THE AMERICAN METHOD

The first style I will describe is the American method, or the zigzag method, most commonly used in the U.S. Hold the handle of the fork in your left palm with your index finger along the back of the fork, tines facing down. While holding your food with the fork, hold the knife in the palm of your right hand (if you're right-handed) with index finger guiding it as you cut one bite of food at a time. (Reverse this if left-handed)

When finished cutting, place the knife on the edge of the plate, sharp edge toward you, and move the fork to your right, or dominant hand, to take the bite with tines up. While the fork is in your right hand, you may scoop or stab anything on your plate. To help guide food onto the fork, you may use your knife or a piece of bread as a *pusher.*

THE CONTINENTAL METHOD

HOW TO USE THE CONTINENTAL METHOD

The Continental or European style of holding and using utensils is very interesting and utilitarian.

While holding the utensils in the same manner as the American method, you cut the bite. Keep the fork in your left hand with fork tines down and take the bite by guiding the fork to your mouth—all the while with tines facing down. You may push food onto the back of the fork as well. You may keep the knife in your right hand awaiting the next cut or place it on the edge of the plate--sharp edge pointed toward you. (Reverse this if left-handed)

If you would like to stab or scoop food, you may use the fork in either hand. However, it is *most* proper to scoop food with fork tines down and using the knife or bread as a pusher.

EATING SOUP

It doesn't matter which method you use for fork and knife. Soup is eaten the same manner.

While eating soup hold your *larger* spoon as you would a pencil. Scoop the soup away from you filling the bowl of the spoon no more than ¾ full. Bring the spoon to the lips and pour the liquid into your mouth. However, do not put the entire spoon into the mouth. Return the spoon to the bowl or the plate underneath. It is proper to tip the bowl to get the last of the soup, but never pick the bowl up to drink. And, never slurp.

BASIC TIPS

- Hold your *larger* spoon as a pencil to eat soup.
- Scoop the soup away from you.
- Never place a utensil on the table after it is used.
- Everyone should have food on his plate before starting to eat.

CHAPTER THREE
BODY LANGUAGE & TABLE
CONVERSATION

BODY LANGUAGE

Body language is so very important in everything we do, because our body language speaks for us. It is an indication of how we feel about ourselves, those around us, and about our environment. So please, be attentive to the way you sit at the table.

So, what is the proper body language at the table? We do not slouch, rock, or tip in your chair. Instead, we sit up straight, but relaxed and not stiff. Alternately, don't sit *overly* stiff as it is possible to dribble food all over the front of us. We lean forward slightly from our *hips* when taking a bite—bringing the food to our mouth, not our mouth to our food.

Returning to the subject of tipping and rocking in our chairs, I have a very good friend who is quite stout. Recently, he joined us for a nice brunch, and because he is quite large, he bent one of my chairs by merely tipping back. I was so embarrassed for him, but thankfully, he did not notice the chair. It would have ruined our enjoyable afternoon.

What kind of grooming would you imagine would be allowed at the table? Trick question! There is no grooming at the table, including picking your teeth, cleaning your nails, combing your hair and apply makeup at the table.

If there is something stuck in your teeth, excuse yourself to the restroom. Additionally, even though some restaurants may provide toothpicks – at a counter by the door – (*I wish it wasn't so*) these are not for use at the table or for use in the presence of others. Using a toothpick has the same visual effect as flossing at the table.

Finally, our last reminder speaks to those whose heads are always so cold that wearing their hats to the table seem appropriate. Don't. Just please remember what your first-grade teacher probably told you every day. Don't wear your hats indoors, *especially* at the table

RULES TO REMEMBER

- No hats at the table.
- Do not apply makeup, clean fingernails, or comb hair at the table.

TABLE CONVERSATION

Our basic instinct at the table is to share, so it follows that conversation is important. Conversations should be pleasant, never argumentative and should include everyone equally. Humor is usually welcome; however, degrading jokes are not.

Keep the conversation light, talk about the day, current life events and friends. Avoid discussions other might find displeasing, if not disgusting, like foot fungus.

This is also a great opportunity to introduce to children the rule of not interrupting others. We want a peaceful setting in which to enjoy the meal and the company of others.

The pace of consuming food slows as we share pleasant conversation, as if we are "savoring the flavor." If you find that you tend to rush through your meal, perhaps savoring the flavor could be your new motto. Others should not feel obliged to rush through their meal to catch up with you. Be considerate, slow it down and enjoy the company and the meal you share.

Please

- No ethnic humor, disgusting topics, politics or religion.
- No discussions of bodily functions.

CHAPTER FOUR
STYLES OF MEALS

FORMALITY MATTERS

There are three styles of meals, two of which are formal. One style of formal meals is courses brought out on platters and in bowls and served to the guests. The second is very formal. Food is plated in the kitchen and placed in front of each diner.

Informal dinners are often served family style, which means food is placed on the table in serving bowls and plates. Food is passed from the left to the right to avoid a traffic – or food – jam, and a disorganized mess. When eating family style, assist the person on your right by holding the bowl or plate after making sure the diner on your left has served himself. Please watch your serving size to make sure that there is enough food for everyone.

FAMILY STYLE MEALS

- Begin when the host begins.

- Serve yourself after the person on your left has served herself.

- Assist the person on your left and right with their serving.

- Pass the pepper with the salt.

FORMAL MEALS

Formal dinners may be plated in the kitchen and served to each diner. Alternately, servers may offer each diner servings from trays and bowls. In both cases, the meal will be served from the left, so lean slightly to assist the server.

If the meal is brought out on trays and bowls, you need to work a bit. With meat or anything served on a tray that cannot be stabbed, slide the serving spoon under the item while steadying it with the serving fork – *hopefully* -- guiding it successfully to your plate. When served vegetables or any food that can be scooped, use the serving spoon to scoop an appropriate serving on to your plate. If there is a sauce or gravy, use the ladle or pour directly from the gravy boat (pitcher) onto meat, rice, or potatoes.

FORMAL MEAL RULES

- Enter the dining room when asked.

- Locate your place card and stand behind that chair until everyone has entered.

- A menu card may be on your plate or between diners.

- There will be salt and pepper for each diner or for every two.

- Finger bowls: dip fingers and dry on your napkin.

CHAPTER FIVE

DINING OUT

DINING OUT BASICS

I would like to tell you a little story, true of course, about why and how I decided to teach and then write about this subject.

While dining out, my husband and I witnessed a young boy, approximately ten, playing soccer with a straw while his father was sitting only a few feet away from him. No kidding. It seemed as if he was trying to see how high he could kick it. I could almost hear the cheers of the crowd. While Father saw what Mr. Soccer was doing, I don't believe he found fault in his son's actions, as he did nothing. I thought, "What a terrible loss of a teachable moment". Dad should have known that a restaurant is no place for a soccer game.

When we visit a restaurant, any type of restaurant, we are just visiting. We need to show respect for property, other diners and those who work there. Please treat the waitstaff with respect; they are people, not just fixtures.

A reservation at a restaurant is a promise to show up at a certain time. Therefore, punctuality is paramount; it is not respectful to the proprietors if you waste their time by arriving late. If you have not made a reservation, please ask politely for inclusion. Pushy, elitist behavior or attitudes are rude and not acceptable behavior no matter how important this dinner may be.

Once you are seated and receive your menus, try to choose quickly. This does not mean you cannot talk to your companions.

Just try to consider that the waitstaff has others to serve. Ask about specials, including prices, and any ingredients of which you are unsure. It is much better to take the time to be sure what is in your meal before receiving it, rather than be disappointed and need to send it back.

If you are a guest, wait for the host to mention what he is ordering. He may want to order a bottle of wine and want to pair it with the food. Additionally, perhaps this meal is meant to be on the *light* side so you would not want to order too much. In any case, it is always best to order mid-priced choices. In addition, please thank the host for the invitation.

If you are the host and you want your guest to know he may order anything, mention that there are wonderful first courses that he may wish to try. You may want to comment about the luscious desserts.

Conversation is as important as the meal you share. So, as you converse, place your utensils on your plate in an upside-down V shape. Usually, the waitstaff recognizes this as a rest in the meal. However, when you are finished with the meal, place your utensils parallel to each other on the right side of the plate. This is the sign for your waitstaff to retrieve the setting.

GENTLE REMINDERS

- Stay in your seat; if you are with a child, remind him also.

- No loud noises, only quiet tones.

- Act respectfully of other's spaces; be mindful of your coat and bags.

- No electronic devices: phones or game boy.

- Use proper table manner.

- Be on time for reservations.

- Model kind behavior toward staff.

- Wear appropriate clothing.

- Always think of others and how your actions will affect them.

Please remember to use all the table manners and etiquette we have discussed. Now, go forth and spread good table manners.

CHAPTER SIX
FINGERS, FORK AND KNIFE

COMMON FINGER FOODS

- Artichoke

- Asparagus

- Bacon, if it is crisp

- Sandwiches

- Cookies

- Small fruit or berries with stems

- French fries and potato chips

- Hamburgers and hot dogs

- Corn on the cob

- Caviar

- Pickles

- Olives

- Tacos

HOW DO I EAT THESE?

Apples:

Quarter apples with a fruit knife or steak knife; the core is cut away from each piece and pieces are eaten with the fingers. If you choose to remove the skin, pare each piece separately.

Artichoke:

Eat artichokes with the fingers one leaf at a time. Dip leaves into the sauce provided. Eat the fleshy part of the leaf, scraping it off between your teeth. Place the leaf on the side of your plate. Remove the choke, the small leaves with sharp points, with your spoon and add to the eaten leaves. Cut the heart into sections using a fork and knife, and dip with the fork into the sauce to eat.

Asparagus:

At a formal dinner, use a fork and knife, cutting one bite at a time. Individual tongs may be used at a *very* formal dinner. In casual settings, asparagus is a finger food if firm and not in a sauce.

Bananas:

At a *formal meal*, peel the banana with fork and knife, eating one bite at a time. However, a whole banana would not be served at a formal meal. Thus, you would eat each smaller piece with a fork and knife. For informal meals, use your hands.

Barbecued Meats:

Barbeque is informal. Hot dogs, hamburgers, ribs and small chicken pieces are treated as finger food. To eat steak, fish, and large chicken pieces, use a fork and steak knife, cutting one bite at a time. Add sauce to your plate, if desired.

Berries:

In a formal setting, a strawberry fork may be used—just spear. If they have a stem, it is finger food. Ladle the sauce or cream onto your fruit plate before dipping.

Bread and Butter:

Break off a small piece of bread, place butter onto the bread plate using a butter knife. Use your knife to spread butter onto bread.

Caviar:

Caviar is finger food. Use the caviar spoon, usually small and round, and place a small amount on your plate or triangular toast that is usually served with caviar. If condiments are served, such as chopped onion, place a small amount on top of the caviar.

Cheese:

Spread soft cheeses such as Brie with the knife provided onto crackers or bread. With firmer cheeses, use the knife to slice a piece and place it onto your plate.

Cherry Tomatoes:

Cherry tomatoes are finger foods, unless it is served in a salad or other entrée. Break the skin in your mouth before chewing. If they are served in a salad or other dish, cut and eat using the fork. Prick the skin to allow the juice to run first to avoid a messy juice explosion.

Chicken:

Never eat chicken with the fingers in a formal dining situation. In an informal setting, you can eat the smaller pieces with the fingers unless it is in a sauce. Larger pieces, such as chicken breasts must be cut using a place or steak knife.

Clams and Oysters:

While holding the shell in one hand and fork in the other, spear the clam, dip it in the sauce and eat it in one bite. You may suck the clam or oyster off the shell at an informal setting.

Condiments:

Place the condiments on to your plate before adding to a food item.

Corn on the Cob:

This is an informal food and is never served at a formal event. Eat with your fingers.

Crackers for Soup:

Place crackers for soup onto the bread plate. Break up into pieces and scatter into the soup.

Grapes:

Snap off a cluster, place on your plate and eat one at a time with fingers.

Lobster:

Pull the meat out with cocktail fork and dip it into melted butter or any sauce that is provided. Eat the tail meat by pulling out one piece at a time. If you pull out a particularly large piece, cut it with your dinner knife or fork before dipping.

Place the empty shell pieces onto a separate waste bowl or plate.

Melon:

At informal meals, melon is considered a finger food; however, it should be eaten with a fork and knife at other times.

Mussels:

Spear mussel, dip in sauce and eat it.

Oranges or Another Citrus:

In formal meals, cut off top and bottom, and slice off peel. Eat segments with fingers or fork and knife. For informal meals, peel with your hands.

Papaya:

Cut papaya in half; take out seeds with spoon, placing seeds on the side of plate. Eat with a fork or spoon.

Peas:

Scoop onto your fork or push using bread or your knife. Never guide with your finger.

Pizza:

Eat with a fork and knife unless the slices are firm.

Salad:

It is always best to use both a fork and knife.

Shish Kabob:

Hold the shish kabob in one hand and use the dinner fork to remove the pieces with the other. Place the stick on the side of the plate. Eat with a fork and knife.

Shrimp:

Small shrimp may be dipped into cocktail sauce using the cocktail fork. Eat large shrimp with fork and knife and place sauce on plate.

Snails/Escargot:

Pick up one at a time using tongs and remove with a cocktail fork—dip into butter.

Soups:

Eat clear soup with a small, round spoon, never filling more than 75% full. Eat from the side of the spoon, never placing the entire spoon into your mouth.

A cream soup is served with a medium round spoon, chunky soups with a large round spoon, and an oval spoon is used for all types of soup and some desserts.

A cup with handle may be picked up and drunk. Never pick up a bowl to drink the soup and never slurp. Place the spoon on the side of the plate when finished.

Spaghetti:

Never cut pasta with fork and knife. Use a fork and twirl until the strands are firmly wrapped around the fork. If there are strands dangling from the fork, take the bite allowing the strands to fall to the plate, use the fork to guide the strands.

Sushi:

Sushi may be eaten with the fingers or chopsticks.

CHAPTER SEVEN
BUSINESS MEAL ETIQUETTE

KNOW BEFORE YOU GO!

SOCIAL MANNERS VS BUSINESS MANNERS

"Good manners will open doors that the best education cannot." Clarence Thomas

The manners we use in social situations are different from those we use in business situations. This is important to note for all business situations. For example, men open doors for women socially; yet in the business world, we open doors for everyone.

In the past, a man was introduced to a woman when in social situations--not so in business. Rank is more significant in business. Thus, we always introduce people to the higher-ranking person first: "Mr. or Ms. Higher Ranked, I would like to introduce *to you* Mr. or Ms. Lesser Rank. Gender is not an issue.

Subsequently, when introducing your manager to a new employee, say the manager's name first and then the new employee. For example, "Ms. Gutierrez, I would like to introduce to you, our newest employee, Ralph Brown."

A client is considered most important or the highest rank. Say the client's name first and then your manager's name if you are introducing your client to your manager. For example, "Ms. Applegate, I would like to introduce to you, our manager, Ms. Gutierrez."

In social situations, people may or may not extend their hands signaling a wish to shake hands. In business, everyone shakes hands, although we typically wait for the most senior people to extend his/her hand first. We grip the other person's hand with equal pressure using a dry right hand.

If seated while being introduced, stand. Smile and shake hands firmly, while maintaining good eye contact. Repeat the other person's name and greet him or her with, "It is so nice to meet you."

GENDER ETIQUETTE

- In business, there is no gender preference.

- Treating a woman as we would in a social setting could be viewed as gratuitous and demeaning.

RESTAURANT MEALS

Table manners are essential so don't leave them at home.

A dear friend shared a story with me about a dinner he had attended with his coworkers and boss. Usually during these typically pleasant dinners, many tasks were accomplished. However, one of these dinners included a new employee who surprised the group with his atrocious table manners making everyone uncomfortable. Thus, not much was accomplished that evening and he was dismissed the next day. Message: don't be that guy!

If you are the first to arrive for a business meal at a restaurant, choose a chair in the center of the table, unless you are the highest ranking, a special client or guest. My first choice is to wait for the others to arrive. This is the best way to ensure that you do not step on anyone's shoes—or sit in his chosen seat.

First impressions are imperative, and meals may be the first-time business associates meet you. So, focus on your body language. Sit tall, not too stiffly and do not rock or tip back in your chair. Do not comb your hair, pick at your teeth, or apply makeup, even if you are alone at the table at the time.

Wait for everyone to arrive and seated before placing your napkin in your lap. Most likely, you will stand to shake hands and your napkin could fall to the floor. Besides, you may appear too eager to eat.

Good conversational skills are critical; business is rarely the only topic discussed. Become well rounded by studying current news and cultural events. Humor is welcome at the table, but ethnic or questionable jokes are not. Do not dominate the conversation, allow others their input, and remember that we share at the table. Keep the conversation light and friendly and watch your language.

When it is time to order, listen to what the host is ordering and try to order something similar if being treated. It wouldn't be appropriate to order a full meal only to find that everyone else is ordering a small salad.

If this is an interview meal, listen to what is being ordered and *again* order similarly. Do not order any item that could splatter on your clothes like pasta in a light broth. You wouldn't want anything that could distract you from the interview. Avoid foods that would get your hands messy; for example, shrimp in the shell.

Chicken breasts or fish with vegetables is always a perfect choice because they are easy to cut and eat. Salads are a good choice too if you cut the vegetables into small bites and are careful about the dressing. Perhaps ask for the dressing to be presented on the side. Avoid alcohol even if everyone else is imbibing. You can celebrate later if you get the job.

TAKE YOUR TABLE MANNERS

Now is the real test of your skills. The food has arrived, and your napkin is in your lap. Which utensil do you use? Choose the outermost fork or spoon. Use the fork to stab or scoop solid food items. Alternately, to scoop a liquid, use the spoon.

TABLE MANNERS REFRESHER

As you remember from an earlier chapter, hold your fork in your non-dominant hand (usually left) tines down, index finger along the spine. While holding the food with the fork, cut one bite at a time with the knife in the palm of your right hand and your index finger guiding it. Place the knife on the edge of the plate, sharp edge toward you and transfer the fork to your right hand to pick up the bite.

This is the American Method—widely used in the United States. I won't mention the Continental method here, but it would be beneficial to read about it again.

Eat soup by picking up the larger spoon (on the far right) and hold it similarly to a pencil. Scoop the soup away from you.

There are a few absolute *don't (s)* we should revisit, especially since our manners will be scrutinized on a business meal. We never eat with our elbows sticking out as if we are flying and never return a used utensil to the table. Instead, place it on the edge of the plate, and we eat only one bite at a time. The table manners our elders taught us years ago are still in vogue; please use them.

Also, say please and thank you when appropriate. Say excuse me when temporarily leaving the table or when coughing and sneezing. If you have a cough or sneeze attack, excuse yourself from the table until your spell in under control.

Never use your napkin to blow your nose; use it only to blot your mouth. Moreover, do so before drinking. It is unsightly to have food or grease on the lip of a glass.

Eat with your mouth closed and don't talk until you have finished the bite. Do not hover over your food; instead lean forward slightly to take a bite. While taking a bite, do not use your finger to guide the food onto your fork.

When bread is on the table, it is fine to help yourself once the entrée has arrived. Never reach over a tablemate; ask for the bread to be passed. Place the bread on the bread plate (yours would be above your forks) or your entree plate. If you use butter, place this on your plate. Tear a small piece of bread, butter it, and eat one piece at a time. Try not to take the last piece of bread if not everyone has had a piece.

Be kind to those around you. Remember to include all in the conversation and smile. Also, remember to be kind to the waitstaff. When you are kind to everyone at the table and then treat the waitstaff as though they are below you, you are exhibiting a disturbing contrast. You may be perceived as a person who treats others kindly in order to further your own agenda. This type of behavior creates distrust.

At the end of the meal, thank the host if you have been treated. If not, you should have calculated your portion as you ordered. Leave the appropriate amount including a fifteen percent tip. Do not make everyone wait as you are trying to figure out your total. If you are the host, pay the bill as quickly as possible to avoid any awkwardness. Now place your napkin on the right side of the plate and thank everyone for the fine discussion.

As you may have noticed, the etiquette we use for business meals is no different from any other situation.

Note

- Always use your best behavior and turn your cellphone off!
- Dress appropriate for the occasion.
- A business meal is never about the food.
- Take a cough or sneeze attack away from the table.
- Blow your nose away from the table.
- Blot your mouth before taking a drink.
- Don't push food onto your fork with your finger.
- Don't discuss business before the first course has arrived.
- Watch your host for table manners clues.
- Do not offer your business card unless someone asks for it.

BUFFET & COCKTAIL RECEPTIONS

"There is no accomplishment so easy to acquire as politeness, and none so profitable.
"George Bernard Shaw

Many times, a business meal could be buffet style with several people with whom you are expected to mingle, which can be very stressful to the mingling skills disadvantaged. A cocktail reception is another potential minefield. Here we will discuss these two situations. The suggestions are the same for both.

First, you may be faced with the ubiquitous nametag. Most people place it on their left shoulder, which seems appropriate because most are right-handed, and this seems the easiest to maneuver. However, the correct position is on your right shoulder.

There is an excellent reason for this. We shake hands with our right hand. The person shaking your hand will first glance at your face, your nametag (because it is in his eye-line), and finally your hand. He will then glance at your nametag again when he finishes shaking your hand. This is great face/name recognition in your favor.

It is best not to arrive hungry. Remember, this event is more about mingling and networking than eating. Yet, you will most probably want to sample the buffet. Please do this as soon as you arrive.

It is best not to arrive hungry. Remember, this event is more about mingling and networking than eating. Yet, you will probably want to sample the buffet. Please do this as soon as you arrive.

It is best if plates and forks are available, but it isn't always the case. If so, try to choose items that you can eat with one bite using your fork. If there are no forks or plates, use a napkin and toothpicks. Arrange no more than two items on your napkin and eat those with your toothpick.

Please do not stand at the buffet table and eat. Walk away and return for a couple more items. However, please do not spend much more than 10-15 minutes eating.

Please keep your glass in your left hand to keep your right hand dry.

Mingling is a focal point of these events. Therefore, it is important to brush up on your mingling skills. Approach those whose body language seems to signal openness and introduce yourself. Most importantly, treat everyone as though that person is special.

The purpose of small talk is to find something in common and create a bond. This is best accomplished by listening, being observant, and asking pertinent questions. *Listen more than talk.*

Honor everyone's personal space and disposition. Avoid intense conversations and weighty discussions, such as marriage, politics, or religion. Maintain good eye contact and watch your body language.

CONVERSATION TOPICS

Before the affair, think of at least three topics. Spend 5-10 minutes talking to one person and move on. If possible, learn something about the guests so you are better prepared to ask pertinent questions. Avoid excess giggling, throat clearing or keeping your hands in your pockets.

- *Good:* Current events, work, books, sports

- *Not:* Religion, sex, politics, illness, cursing or gossip

EATING AND DRINKING

- Use a napkin if you are carrying food.

- Eat quickly and do not hold court at the buffet table.

- Do not eat and drink at the same time.

- Try to arrange food on your plate in a way that it will be easy to eat in one bite.

- Use toothpicks if available.

- Keep drink in left hand; no alcohol.

CHAPTER EIGHT
SUSHI ETIQUETTE

For those who wish to eat sushi properly and not insult the
chef

WHY SUSHI ETIQUETTE?

To those who love sushi, stating that it is popular is stating the obvious. Obvious and true. It is especially popular, not only in the US, but in many parts of the world. It is consumed on dates, the quick lunch, and more importantly during business meals. Therefore, I felt compelled to write a short, but concise chapter on the etiquette of eating sushi. Additionally, another factor was the numerous appeals from clients for just such a resource.

Of course, considering the etiquette of eating sushi, it may be best to also read the following chapter on chopstick etiquette.

Enjoy your sushi!

INSULT THE CHEF?

Sushi etiquette is evolving quite quickly; so quickly, in fact, that there are few non-debatable absolutes. Some heartily believe in mixing wasabi with the soy sauce, while some argue it insults the abilities of the chef. We will explore this subject and even more interesting discrepancies as we move forward.

Let's begin at the beginning: deciding where to sit when entering a sushi restaurant. Sitting at the sushi bar is quite a treat and requires just a bit more etiquette than if seated at a table. For example, if wishing to use the most proper etiquette, it is expected to ask those seated if the seats are available. This is most respectful to those seated. Moreover, since he/she is working at the counter, it is also most proper to consider what may or may not insult the sushi chef or itamae. More on this later.

ETIQUETTE, PROCEDURES, AND THE "WHYS"

Most sushi is finger food, but many westerners use chopsticks. Both methods are fine but should be done correctly. Because it is viewed as a finger food, a towel (oshibori) is presented to the diner to clean the hands. Fold it back neatly after using. You may leave it to the left, next to the plate for finger wiping.

In front of each diner is a little cup or saucer for soy sauce of which it is impolite to fill fully. Fill no more than one third. More appears wasteful and disrespectful to the chef, as if he/she isn't capable of seasoning properly. This is very important to note when sitting at the sushi counter where the chef is in full view of the diner's actions.

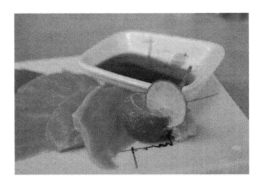

Sashimi is typically served first and is eaten with chopsticks. Most agree that a bit of wasabi should or could be added to the soy sauce for the sashimi, of which it is dipped. However, when sitting at the counter, it may be insulting to the chef. Therefore, adding a bit of wasabi to the meat first and then dipping in the sauce might be best.

Adding the wasabi to the sauce is in direct contrast to what some believe is proper for sushi eating. Some firmly believe that it is disrespectful and unnecessary to mix wasabi into the soy sauce, while some drone on and on about it being the only way to enjoy it, as if sushi wouldn't taste as good without *extra* wasabi.

This is the key here. If one enjoys more wasabi than is typically found in sushi, it is most polite to ask the chef to add more into the rolls or pieces. However, if one absolutely needs more wasabi, it is viewed as most polite to add a bit to the roll. If adding it to the soy sauce, it should be a very small amount.

SUSHI AND MORE SUSHI

Not all sushi is created equal. There are absolute differences in quality, but for the sake of this little ditty, types are most important to discuss here, because there is a slightly different etiquette involved with each.

Nigiri (seasoned rice topped with fish or another topping) may be dipped in sauce—fish side down. However, if it has a glaze on it, it has already been seasoned. It is appropriate, though, to take some of the ginger (always served with sushi as a palette cleanser), dip it into the sauce with chopsticks, and brush the nigiri with it.

Gunkan (small cups made of sushi rice and dried seaweed which is filled with seafood or other ingredients) may be treated the same or soy sauce may be poured over it. The same goes for the taco or cone version of sushi: temaki.

Of course, the popular sushi roll westerners tend to enjoy, norimaki, or inside out sushi, is dipped using chopsticks.

Seasoned, glazed, nigiri. No soy sauce is needed.

LET'S EAT!

Now, on to eating sushi. If using the fingers, pick up a piece of nigiri with the index finger at the short side farthest from you and middle finger along the long side, so your palm would be "over" the sushi and the thumb on the opposite long side. Next< lift it up and flip it upside down. The fish is now on the bottom of the sushi and can be dipped into the soy sauce. Turn the wrist so that the fish is facing you.

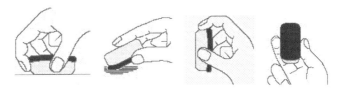

Pictures found on Nifty.com—how to eat sushi

Interestingly, it is considered perfect sushi eating to incline the head back and *somewhat* "toss" the piece in the mouth so that the fish is touching the tongue. This might take practice for some.

Although considered appropriate, for many of us these pieces are much too large to be eaten in one bite. What to do? If we bite it in half, it may fall apart. Of course, this might be the only choice if the bite really is too large for us. Nevertheless, there is nothing wrong with asking for the sushi to be made smaller. This is not an insult. However, this must be done before the sushi is made. If we do bite it in half, we hold onto the piece in between bites. It is not returned to the plate.

Using chopsticks to eat sushi is done similarly to using the fingers. Grip the nigiri firmly and turn it on its side (fish is pointing to the side); then while holding it sideways (one stick on the fish side and one on the rice side) turn the wrist so that the fish is facing down when dipping. A little bit of the rice may be dipped as well, but not much. It will fall apart.

Pictures found on Nifty.com--how to eat sushi

CHAPTER NINE
CHOPSTICK ETIQUETTE

THE BASICS

As we would never clean our hosts' utensils in their presence, the same is true of chopsticks. No rubbing them together.

Hold your chopsticks towards their end, not in the middle or the front third.

Place them parallel to yourself on the holder, with the tips to the left, (shoyu dish—most respectful) when not in use and return them to the original wrapper when finished with the meal.

If seated at a sushi bar, the chopsticks are placed parallel to the edge of the bar with the narrow ends on the chopstick rest or across your plate—never lean them on your plate.

The broad end is used to pick up sushi, or any other food, from a communal dish or to place food to another's dish. Never use the narrow ends that are used for eating to choose communal food to share.

Don't pass food from one set of chopsticks to another. This practice resembles a Japanese funeral ritual.

Never stick and leave chopsticks in food, especially rice, as it too resembles part of a funeral ritual.

These are not weapons. Do not spear or stab food with them. Additionally, never point, wave, play, or move dishes with them.

With large pieces of food, separate by cutting with the chopsticks: exert pressure in the center of the piece while tearing the two pieces apart. It is somewhat like a reverse scissors' movement. It is also acceptable to pick up the entire piece with your chopsticks and take a bite.

DO (S) AND DON'T (S)

- Do ask what is freshest, but not if it is fresh.

- Do ask about specials or anything that may not be on the menu.

- Do not eat the ginger with the sushi. It is a palette cleanser to eat in between sushi pieces.

- Do not pour too much soy sauce in your dish.

- Do not disassemble sushi.

- When offered soup with no spoon, drink from the bowl. Guide the noodles to the mouth with chopsticks.

- Burping is impolite.

- Drink sake before or after the meal. The reasoning is that they are both rice products, thus don't mix well.

- Green tea or beer is thought to be a better accompaniment with sushi.

- Cold sake is higher quality than hot.

- When with others, pour drinks for them, as it is considered loutish to pour for oneself. Always watch their glasses and refill them. They will do the same. If they don't, finish the drink, and while holding the glass, lean it toward them slightly.

- Kanpai! (empty your cup) is the appropriate toast, but never use "chin-chin" as it refers to male genitalia.

- The itamae never touches money when handling food. The tip may be left in a jar, with wait staff, or on the bill.

Knives and forks may be used in high-end western restaurants only if offered.

CHAPTER TEN
HOW TO TEA—BRITISH TEA TIMES

A SPOT OF HISTORY

"Tea is quiet and our thirst for tea is never far from our craving for beauty."

James Norwood Pratt

Let's begin with a bit of tea history and how tea became so popular in Britain. Tea arrived and is first sold through a popular coffee house, Thomas Garway's Coffee House in Exchange Alley, London in 1658.

(For more information about Thomas Garway and that time period, please visit, Tsiosophy.com.)

In 1664, Charles II of England received a gift of tea from the British East India Company, which was the largest trading company in the world at the time. His consort, Catherine de Braganza from Portugal, who enjoyed tea in her homeland, serves tea to the ladies of the English court. As a result, it became very popular with the aristocracy.

Of course, with all this drinking and enjoying, one must have special pots in which to serve it. So, the first silver teapots were crafted in 1670. Later, Josiah Wedgwood, in 1765, creates his Queen's Ware (for Queen Charlotte), which is mass-produced earthenware that is resistant to heat and sets the standard for tea ware.

NOTE

What follows are the British tea times, traditional teas served and accompaniments.

TEA TIMES

BREAKFAST TEA

Before the 1700's ale was the breakfast beverage of choice. It was Queen Anne (1665-1714) who influenced the people of the day with her love of tea to incorporate tea drinking into their everyday lives.

TYPICAL TEA CHOICES

- English Breakfast.
- Irish Breakfast.
- Ceylon Breakfast.

These are strong teas from India and Ceylon with an extra caffeine kick.

TYPICAL FOOD CHOICES

- Quick breads with herbs.
- Toast and butter.
- Waffles.

LOW TEA OR AFTERNOON TEAS—4 PM

It was around 1840, the dear friend of Queen Victoria, Duchess Anna of Bedford, began feeling faint in the afternoons. Thus, she started sipping tea into the dinner hour. It soon became a shared experience with her friends having tea and snacks. Thus, the public began to sit for tea in the afternoon as well.

Queen Victoria (1819-1901) further promoted the afternoon tea ritual.

TYPICAL TEA CHOICES

- Ceylon.
- Earl Grey.
- Darjeeling.
- Tea with a Twist.
- Chinese Gunpowder.
- Dragonwell.

TYPICAL FOOD CHOICES

- Bread and butter.

- Cakes.

- Fruit tarts.

- Macaroons.

- Dainty sandwiches.

HIGH TEA—6 PM

Surprisingly, high tea began as a poor working-class ritual. The poor could only afford one meal, which was lunch. Therefore, they would save everything they could stow away during the day, cheese, meats, fish and bread. They would then have tea at home with the leftovers.

As people began to prosper, the tea included a substantial meal: eggs, sausages, fish and mashed potatoes. High tea isn't really practiced in the same manner today. It has been replaced by dinner with tea served afterward.

TYPICAL TEA CHOICES

- Ceylon blended teas.
- Assam blended teas.

TYPICAL FOOD CHOICES

- Biscuits or scones with jam.
- Cheese or meats.

- Light meals, such as eggs and sausages with French fries and peas.

TEA BREAK

Coffee Break? Not in Great Britain. You can expect a tea break. It is 15-30 minutes to relax mid-morning and mid-afternoon with tea and cookies (biscuits).

It began 250 years ago, but many employers thought that the break would make their employees lazy. Luckily, during World War 1, it was found that tea breaks increased the productivity and stamina of employees.

TYPICAL TEA CHOICES

- Earl Grey.
- Lapsang Souchong.
- Orange Pekoe.

TYPICAL FOOD CHOICES

- Shortbreads.
- Sugar cookies.
- Quick breads.

NOTE

Today, many in Great Britain enjoy coffee just as much as they do tea.

NURSERY TEA

Nursery tea is a mid-morning teatime for nursery school children and is sometime called tea party time. The tea is milky and is served with biscuits. I offered this same tea to my children when they were quite young.

Hey, remember the song, "I'm a little teapot"?

TYPICAL TEA CHOICES

- Cambric.
- Vanilla Nursery tea.

TYPICAL FOOD CHOICES

- Tea biscuits.
- Cinnamon rolls.
- Jam cookies.
- Oatcakes.

TEA GARDENS

Finally! The weekend arrives and it's time to relax. Families and couples enjoy Tea Gardens on Sunday. This is a perfect atmosphere for chatting and sipping tea.

TYPICAL TEA CHOICES

- Darjeeling.
- Earl Grey.

TYPICAL FOOD CHOICES

- Cucumber, egg, ham, or watercress sandwiches with no crusts.
- Red salmon mousse in bread rolls.
- Slices from cream-cheese loaves.
- Teacakes.
- Fresh berry tarts.

TEASHOP TEA

Teashops are very popular in England. The first Lyons teashop opened in 1774 in Piccadilly, London. By 1900, there were over 250.

TYPICAL TEA CHOICES

- Ceylon.
- Assam (Orange Pekoe grade).

TYPICAL FOOD CHOICES

- Scones and butter.
- Tea biscuits.
- Crumpets.

HOTEL TEA

What started in the 1700's Roadside Inns to greet weary travelers, hotels of today offer their own tea and tidbits.

The English love their cream—double cream, heavy cream, single cream and cream and enjoy their tea with their favorite used on their choice of treats, which inns are known for.

TYPICAL TEA CHOICES

- Russian Caravan.
- Lapsang Souchong.
- Orange Spice.
- Chinese Scented.

TYPICAL FOOD CHOICES

- Dainty sandwiches.
- Scrumptious desserts, including scones with thick clotted cream.

TEA AT THE RITZ

Toned down from earlier days of anybody whose anybody had to be there, the Ritz is still formal, but not stuffy. Opening in 1906, it has been serving tea from day one. It was also, the first place to allow unescorted women.

TYPICAL FOOD CHOICES

- Finger sandwiches, such as cucumber and anchovies, egg mayonnaise with mustard and watercress.
- Meats, such as ham, smoked salmon, or smoked turkey with sweet mustard.
- Scones with strawberry jam and clotted cream.

Bottom Line: The English drink tea all the time and will make any excuse to ritualize it.

HOW TO BREW TEA

85% of all English use tea bags today, but the infusion method is as popular as it has ever been.

STEPS TO A PERFECT CUP OF TEA

- Wash the teapot with soap and water.
- Warm the teapot with hot water.
- Dry.
- Boil fresh water in another pot—just to the boil.
- Add 1 teaspoon of tealeaves per 6 oz. of boiling water to the teapot.
- Add boiling water to the tea.
- *Always add the water to the leaves.*
- Cover with lid and steep for 3-5 minutes.
- Serve immediately.

Serve from the pot; do not steep in the cup

NOTE

Remove the tea from the pot or the tea will become bitter. Pour the tea into another pot using a strainer. Alternatively, use a pot with a removable strainer basket or use a tea ball (mesh strainers are better infusers). The tea may be strained over the cup using a cup strainer.

Keep boiling water available for seconds.

HOW TO DRINK TEA

Begin with your favorite cup. Add the milk (not cream) or lemon to it. Alternately, you may pour milk in after the tea to assure the correct amount.

The English usually drink their tea with milk because in the early days, the cups were fragile and could crack with addition of hot water. Milk was added to the cups first to decrease the trauma to the cups. One can drink tea straight, white (with milk), or white with sugar.

The host pours tea for her guests. Then you slip your index finger through the handle of the cup, almost up to the first knuckle. Secure it by placing your thumb on the top of the handle, allowing the bottom of the handle to rest on your middle finger. Do not extend the pinkie finger, as it is viewed as gauche.

Add sugar to your tea, with the serving spoon or tongs. Use your spoon to stir your tea, never using the serving spoon. Stir quietly and don't clink the sides of the cup with the spoon. Never leave the spoon in the cup. Do not sip your tea from the spoon. Place it quietly on the saucer, behind the cup on the right-hand side under the handle.

Do not blow on hot tea. Lift the saucer with the cup when seated away from the table or standing. Lift only the cup when seated at the table.

Don't swirl the tea when it is getting low. This is viewed as undignified. Lower your eyes to look into your cup while sipping to avoid spilling. Sip don't slurp.

WITH FOOD

Swallow your food before sipping your tea. Take dainty bites.

When using jam and cream, place them on your plate then your scone. To eat scones, break off a small piece, spread the jam, and then top it with a dollop of cream.

If this is buffet style, never place used plates, cups, napkins, or utensils on the tea table.

TEA PARTY

Special occasions, such as a tea party, require invitations. Send these at least three weeks in advance. Inform your guests what to expect, including the time and place. Finally, prepare the necessary items.

- Teapot—silver pot if it's formal
- China
- Cups and saucers
- Teaspoons
- Sugar bowl or tongs
- Some insist that only cubes be served
- Tea strainer
- Lemon dish and fork
- Serving utensils

Seek help serving if this is a large tea. Always attend to the cups. Your guests may help themselves to the refreshments after the tea has been served.

TEA PARAPHERNALIA

TEA CADDY

Used to store tealeaves. Tea stored in a tightly sealed container, in a cool dry place and will stay fresh up to two years.

TEASPOON

Used to measure the tea. Use one teaspoon per every 6oz of water.

TEA COZY

Artistically crafted cover for the teapot, used to help keep the pot warm.

PASTRY PLATES

Tea service plates, usually small heirloom plates, used as pastry, dessert, cake, and bread and butter plates.

TEABAG TONGS

Used to lift and squeeze tea bags.

STOP BOWL

A plate or bowl designed to hold the bag or ball.

LEMON SQUEEZER

A small gadget that holds a wedge of lemon and squeezes it into the tea without getting juice on one's fingers.

SUGAR TONGS

Used to add sugar cubes to tea, appearing in 1780.

TEA BALL

The mesh balls are better infusers than the perforated. There are big balls or eggs for the pot and small ones for the cup.

STRAINERS

A mesh strainer fits on top of a cup and is used to hold tea leaves. Pour the just-boiling water over it. Alternately, it can be a basket that is placed in a pot to hold the leaves.

GLOSSARY OF TEAS MENTIONED

ENGLISH BREAKFAST

It is a full-bodied, brisk tea with enough caffeine to get you through the morning.

IRISH BREAKFAST

Slightly stronger than English Breakfast, this is a robust, rich and strong tea.

CEYLON BREAKFAST

A Shi Lanka tea, delicate, and golden.

CEYLON BLENDED TEAS

One of my favorite black teas because they tend to be blended carefully to enhance and balance flavors. Earl Grey is a great example.

EARL GREY

A blended tea named **FOR** Earl Grey, the Prime Minister of England from 1830-1834. Originally, it was a gift from a grateful Chinese mandarin. Mr. Grey had it blended (matched) by Twinings and has a citrus scent.

DARJEELING

My absolute favorite if drinking a black tea. This is an Indian black tea with a fine, delicate flavor.

TEA WITH A TWIST

It's exactly as it sounds: tea with a twist of lemon.

CHINESE GUNPOWDER

A Chinese green tea named for the size of its leaf which is close to the size of gunpowder. The name an interesting stark contrast, if you will. Gunpowder elicits the imagine of power, and yet this is a light-bodied tea. Tea trivia can be fun.

DRAGONWELL

A green Chinese tea that is slightly sweet, aromatic and cooling.

ASSAM BLENDED TEAS

An Indian black tea that is pungent, malty, full bodied and dark.

LAPSANG SOUCHONG

A red tea from China, which is amber and slightly acidic, and has a faint smoky taste.

ORANGE PEKOE

This black tea is a blend of Ceylon teas and is the most recognizable grocery store tea. Yet, this doesn't diminish its quality. Typically, it is quite nice.

CAMBRIC

A hot drink for children made of milk, water, sugar and a bit of tea. This was the tea I made for my children when they were young. It made them feel all grown up.

VANILLA NURSERY TEA

This vanilla scented tea is similar to Cambric.

RUSSIAN CARAVAN

This too, is a conundrum. The name implies the tea is from Russia or was grown there. Yet, it is a Chinese dark, robust black tea with a smoky flavor. More than likely, the name originated from the journey in which the tea traveled: from China through Russia to Europe. It's thought to have the 'smoky' flavor from the campfires of the long journey.

ORANGE SPICE

Depending on the tea provider, this black tea scented with orange and spice can have an off-putting strong orange and/or spice flavor or could be well balanced and pleasant. Please don't judge all based on one provider.

Chinese Scented

Ditto on this black tea scented with spices. When you find one you like, it is worth tasting those you give to your least favorite tea-drinking friend.

CHAPTER ELEVEN
WINE ETIQUETTE

WHY WINE ETIQUETTE?

Why would I teach and write about wine etiquette? The decision was as easy as the inspiration. We had just returned from a trip to the Sonoma Valley with wonderful bottles of luscious wines we had tasted and decided that we needed to share with a friend. As we shared the wine, he asked questions about how he should hold the glass, why people smell the cork, and what should he do when someone brings a bottle of wine to dinner. All very excellent questions and I decided at that moment that Bacchus needed help here on earth. Therefore, I designed my Wine Etiquette class and ultimately wrote this chapter.

I wrote this in an easy to read, unpretentious, conversational style. I hope you enjoy reading this as much as I did writing it.

WHERE TO BEGIN?

"The peoples of the Mediterranean began to emerge from barbarism when they learnt to cultivate the olive and the vine." Thucydides, Greek Historian, 5ᵗʰ century BC.

The earliest historical writings, including the bible, referred to making and drinking wine. Many cultures considered wine as important as the food they ate. Many still do. Wine embodies the complexities of life and we share those as we share the wine.

Sharing wine should be enjoyable and stress free. To that end, the etiquette surrounding wine and wine tasting is mostly common sense. So, why discuss wine etiquette? Wine has always been, and most likely will continue to be, the beverage of choice for the business dinner and special occasion meal making the etiquette involved essential knowledge.

However, because of this distinction, there seems to be an aura of snobbery around wine tasting. Some people believe this to be a truism, but it is not. The average person does not spend time judging others while drinking wine; they drink wine to delve into the silky layer thought only to exist in our imagination.

TASTING WINE

Our first step is to develop a procedure for tasting wines. Taste the same style, region, varietal, or quality, so comparisons are easier. On a recent trip traveling the Sonoma valley in California, my husband and I had tried as many Zinfandels as we could. Because we were comparing the same varietal in each winery, it became easier to observe the differences. Good to note, many of those wonderful Zinfandels were from Dry Creek Valley.

Wineries are an excellent place to broaden your wine horizons and knowledge; if you have a chance to visit, please do so. Most of the people behind the counters pouring the wine can help you with your technique and are a great source of information. If visiting a winery is out of the question, invest in a good book, subscribe to periodicals, such as "Wine Spectator" or visit a good website, such as: https://www.thespruceeats.com/.

MY FAVORITE WINE BOOKS

- *The University Wine Course*, by Marian W. Baldy, PhD.

- *The Wine Bible*, by Karen MacNeil.

- *The World Atlas of Wine*, by Hugh Johnson, in fact anything by Mr. Johnson.

- *Love by the Glass*, by Dorothy J. Gaiter and John Brecher.

- *The Taste of Wine*, by Emile Peynaud.

HOLD AND LOOK INTO THE GLASS

For tasting wine, you will need a glass. It should be clear, tulip shaped (to facilitate smelling the wine), and the bowl roomy enough to tip and swirl the wine, ideally 200-230ml. The stem needs to be long enough to hold onto without touching the bowl. It is customary to hold the stem with two fingers and thumb with no extending pinkie. In fact, in some countries it is customary to hold onto the base of the glass to taste.

To this I say, "Be practical!" Many of my friends are older or have dexterity problems due to illness. If they need to hold onto the bowl to *enjoy* the wine, so be it. Tasting a wine requires critical thinking, observation and comparisons, whereas to enjoy the wine we merely drink it.

One of the reasons to hold the glass by the stem is to keep the wine cool. Secondly, you need to look at the wine, and fingerprints *would* obscure your vision during tasting. So, if you can hold the glass correctly, please do so.

No, you are not ready to taste the wine yet—more looking. You are now looking for legs on your glass. Swirl the wine counterclockwise if you are right-handed. As you gaze through the glass, you will see legs or tears streaming down the sides. Supposedly, this tells you the sugar content of the wine, which indicates alcohol and richness. Some sources swear by this and some discount it. I believe more legs indicate a fuller mouthfeel. In addition, swirling incorporates more air into the wine and opens the bouquet.

SMELLING THE WINE

Smelling, or nosing the wine comes next. A short sniff, swirl and sniff again. As the wine *opens* up you should smell its complexities. Take long sniffs every few times and savor the smells. This helps determine the aromas you detect.

In our efforts toward olfactory self-discovery, the aroma wheel invented by Dr. Ann Noble at the University of California is a useful tool and easy to obtain. Visit the web at: http://www.winearomawheel.com/. Included with the wheel, is a packet of information that can be used to create your own aroma fest.

WINE VOCABULARY

An entire vocabulary is involved with the smelling and tasting of wine. In many wine books, you will find a vocabulary index explaining all the different terms. In fact, all my favorite wine books include a glossary of terms.

Some of the terms you will find as you do your research are these that I found on another very helpful website, All Things Corked & Forked Wine School--http://www.vinology.com/wine-terms/. **For example:**

Fining — the addition of egg whites or gelatin (among other things) to clear the wine of unwanted particles.

Malolactic fermentation — a secondary fermentation in which the tartness of malic acid in wine is changed into a smooth, lactic sensation. Wines described as "buttery" or "creamy" have gone through "malo".

Open — tasting term signifying a wine that is ready to drink.

TASTE THE WINE

Finally, we get to taste. Take your first sip and let it flow through your mouth. Ensure to swish the wine around the entire inside of your mouth. Oenophiles call this chewing.

Aerate the wine in your mouth by sucking some air through your lips. This helps bring all the aromas to the olfactory bulb and intensifies the flavors. I can only do this with a tiny sip of wine, as I'm not very coordinated.

You may see professionals tasting wine in this manner and it may look intimidating. Believe me, no one is going to grade you or send you to *wine prison* because you cannot chew the wine. Not having been endowed with coordination, I slosh it around my mouth, and I haven't been thrown out of a winery yet. Wine tasting is supposed to be fun, so enjoy.

Now the fun begins. What flavors do you taste? This skill may take time to develop and you may require assistance identifying the elements. Again, a good book is an asset. With a red wine, you may taste chocolate, cherries, berries or a variety of soft, red fruits.

White wines might possess tropical flavors, such as pineapple. Quite often, they taste like tree fruits, such as lemon, peach or apple. Again, each wine is different, and each taster is an individual. My husband is always frustrated with the labels on wine bottles. He can't taste any of the flavors mentioned. We are all different and we can all improve as we age—like a good bottle of wine.

Taste also identifies body, acidity, length, balance, sweetness, and tannins. Essentially, *body* is how the wine feels in the mouth. It might feel thin and watery or round and full bodied with variances in-between. *Acidity* is easy. Is it soft or tart and refreshing? *Length* simply describes how long the flavors linger. In addition, *balance* is exactly what it implies. Now *sweetness* is a little deceptive; some will taste fruit and feel the wine is sweet. This is not always the case. A wine could have some fruit flavor but could be bone dry, dry, or sweet. *Tannins* are found in red wine and can be very astringent when a wine is young and typically softens as it ages.

TASTING ORDER

The order in which you taste wine is extremely important, so there are rules to help you get the most from wines. Taste dry before sweet because the dry would taste sour after the sweet. Taste the lighter bodied wines, like a Gamay, before a full-bodied wine, like a Cabernet Sauvignon. If you tasted in opposite order, it would be like having the chocolate decadence before the chicken sandwich.

Usually you would taste white before red, as white wines are generally considered lighter bodied than reds.

Finally, taste young before old. As wines age, they tend to become milder and softer as opposed to the lively and possibly 'in your face' quality of the younger wine. If you tasted the older wine first, the younger would taste like sour water.

Note

Do not wear perfume or stand near anyone wearing it or a smoker; it will interfere with your aroma detecting.

Most serious wine tasters spit, only because tasting more than a few wines would dull the palate and cause intoxication. Decide for yourself.

SPARKLING WINES AND CHAMPAGNES

"I drink it when I'm happy and when I'm sad. Sometimes I drink it when I'm alone. When I have company, I consider it obligatory. I trifle with it if I'm not hungry and drink it when I am. Otherwise I never touch it—unless I'm thirsty." Madame Lily Bollinger, House of Bollinger Champagne.

I love that quote; it has the essence of pure joy. I think I could drink sparkling wine every day, if it wasn't for the alcohol.

Why would I use the term sparkling wine and not Champagne? I live in California, so I drink more wines from this area. In France, the wines are named for the region in which the grapes are grown and blended into wine. Champagne is a region in France, so the sparkling wine from that region carries its name.

All good sparkling wines are made in the French fashion called, methode champenoise. This is a time consuming but proven process producing smaller, finer bubbles that last longer, resulting in a more complex and richer taste.

STYLES OF SPARKLERS

- Brut is the driest and most food friendly.

- Extra Dry is sweeter and more approachable for beginners.

- Sec is a sweet style.

- Demi Sec is very sweet; watch out for cavities with this one.

- Cremant is a cross between a still wine and a sparkling wine—fewer bubbles.

- Tete de Cuvee is a blend and the name connotes the best.

I believe most of us have watched old movies with people sipping from saucer-shaped champagne glasses. Some of you may have some in your cupboard; with hope, you are using them as fruit-cocktail glasses. The best Champagne glasses are tulip or flute shaped. The bubbles are free to rise, and the aroma is easier to smell.

Follow the same techniques when tasting sparkling wines as for still wines. First, look at the size, number, and flow of the bubbles. Bubbles are everything with sparkling wine and should flow vertically and constantly.

Secondly, look for color; each sparkler has its own hue or color, which may indicate quality.

Next, smell the wine. You may find lemon, roses, or toast.

Finally, taste. The fruit could be lively or subdued; it could be dry and astringent or sweet and delicate. Every wine is different, so experiment.

RESPECT FOR THE BOTTLE

STORAGE

How you store the bottles you purchase will determine how long your wine will keep. For example, a very good friend purchased a case of excellent wine – placing it in his trunk – at a three-hour function we all attended. Because of the heat, his delicious Fume Blanc turned into a not so wonderful Sherry. It was an expensive lesson.

If you purchase wines during your visit to a winery, remember to store your wine in an ice chest until you get home, or have it shipped.

For home storage, find a cool location, typically in the middle of the home. Keep your wines in a dark, cool (55-60 degrees), humidity-controlled environment (if it is too dry, the cork will dry out and air may enter). However, a constant temperature is much more important than coolness. Fluctuations in temperature would cause the bottle to expand and contract possibly allowing air to enter or wine to seep out. A shallow closet in a cool hallway where the temperature is between 60-65 degrees works fine for me.

The bottles should lie horizontally because the wine should have constant contact with the cork. An old wine box works well; it even has the insert for the bottles. The new screw top bottles may be stored vertically or horizontally.

SERVING TEMPERATURE

To enjoy your wines at their best, serve them at the proper temperature. In the past, conventional wisdom was to serve white wine directly from the refrigerator and red wine at room temperature.

Today, we have become a bit more sophisticated. Most refrigerators are around 32 degrees and a room in central California in the spring is around 80 degrees—much too cold for white and too hot for reds.

RED WINES

Red wines should be slightly cooler than room temperature (60-65 degrees) when served. There are exceptions as in the lighter, fruitier reds. You may prefer these chilled a bit more. Many people chill most of their reds to cellar temperature (55 degrees) and find this best. Experiment and decide for yourself.

TO DECANT OR NOT TO DECANT

With some reds, you might want to decant; harmless organic matter, sediment, may reside in the bottle. Allow the bottle to set upright a few hours, and then slowly pour the wine into a clean, dry vessel.

Even though, at times, reds may seem too tannic or all alcohol, please resist the temptation to decant *all* red wines. Aeration tends to soften and mellow tannic red wine; however, *air destroys wine.* The risk may outweigh the benefit.

WHITE WINES

Serve white wines chilled, but not too cool because the wines will lose their character. Experiment and decide which whites you prefer cold and which just cool. I find that Chardonnay tastes better and the flavors open up when just chilled; in contrast, a Gewürztraminer tastes best cold.

SPARKLING WINES

As for sparkling wines, French sources suggest chilling to 44-50 degrees. However, do not chill your wines, still or sparkling, for more than a few days in a regular refrigerator. The wines may pick up smells or flavors and lose some character. A wine refrigerator may be best or just a cool spot in your home.

OPENING THE BOTTLE

You won't be able to drink wine unless you open the bottle. With the popularity of screw caps, which I love, we do not have to worry about procedure. Nevertheless, until all still wines are bottled with crew cap it's best to discuss the proper procedure of opening the bottle.

Still wines are fairly cut and dry. Acquire a good corkscrew and foil cutter and the rest is a breeze. First, cut the foil under the lip of the bottle and peel it off. Then wipe off the top of the bottle with a clean cloth. Next, using the corkscrew, remove the cork, carefully. There may be sediments on the cork, so you want to avoid dropping those into the bottle, if possible. Wipe the inner lip of the bottle. Finally, pour the wine into clean, dry glasses. Wipe off the lip of the bottle to avoid dripping the wine after pouring.

Opening sparkling wines take a bit more finesse. Strip the foil off the top of the bottle, carefully undo the wire while holding onto the cork, and tilt the bottle at a 45-degree angle holding the cork with a towel draped over the bottle. With your other hand, turn the bottle while easing the cork out. Pour no more than half of a glass and enjoy. Above all, avoid the loud pop and spray portrayed in movies.

Note

- Red wines benefit from a slight chill and whites open up as they warm a bit.

DINING OUT

ORDERING WINE

Ordering wine in a restaurant can be intimidating. Actually, just looking at the wine list can be overwhelming. However, there are steps we can take to make this task much easier.

HOW TO CHOOSE A WINE

The first step is to take a deep breath and realize that you don't have to know about every wine on the list.

Ask questions and take into consideration what you are eating. Decide if you want white or red—you have just eliminated half of the list. Eliminate any wines that are not within your price range.

You may even ask to have a small taste of a wine to help you make up your mind. Many times, I will mention that we are learning about wines and ask for suggestions. If you are adventurous, ask the sommelier to match the wines with each course. *That is an experience.*

YOUR WINE HAS ARRIVED—NOW WHAT?

When your wine arrives, check the label to make sure it is what you ordered. A '09 vintage is not the same as a '11.

The waiter will open the bottle and place the cork next to the person who ordered the wine. You may sniff it if you care to, but it doesn't tell you much. I love the smell of the cork, so I do. If it smells like vinegar, the wine is bad.

Roll the cork between your fingers to check the moistness and condition of the cork. It should be moist indicating contact between cork and wine. If it is not wet, air could have gotten into the bottle and ruined it. If the cork is crumbling, the wine could have gone bad. Nevertheless, tasting the wine is the true test.

THE POUR

The waiter will pour a little wine into the host's glass. If the wine is good, say so. He will then pour for the others at the table and finish with the host.

If you don't like the wine, sorry it's yours. Hence, decide if you want to order another one or just drink this one. You pay for both.

There are only three instances when it is appropriate to refuse a wine and send it back. These include wines that are corked, vinegary, or taste like bad sherry.

CORKED WINE—CORK TAINT

A corked wine smells like old wet socks and tastes just as bad. You will know as soon as you smell the wine. The restaurant should allow an exchange because this is a problem with the cork. We acquire corked bottles from the grocery store quite often. It happens. If the restaurant does not allow the exchange, you have no recourse except to never return.

OXIDIZED WINE—VINEGAR ATTRIBUTES

Vinegar is vinegar and you will recognize the odor. Wine does not smell or taste like this unless it is bad. This is a winery problem; so typically, we shouldn't order a bottle of the same wine. However, it could just be a problem with the cork. Why risk it though. Your waiter should have no problem exchanging it for you.

COOKED WINE—SHERRY ATTRIBUTES

A wine that tastes a bit like sherry and appears darker than it should be has been stored incorrectly. This is a problem with the restaurant or their supplier, not you. Therefore, the waiter *should* bring you another bottle of something else, no excuses. Order something younger with the hope that it hasn't had enough time to be damaged.

Often you may find cork in your luscious liquid. Please avoid the temptation to put your finger in the glass to retrieve it; use your spoon or a napkin.

Returning now to how we hold the glass. Some restaurants have such big glasses that I have trouble holding onto the stem without spilling the entire glass on me. If you need to hold onto the bowl of the glass, do it. Any rule that lessens the joy of the wine experience is not a good rule.

Note

- A good tip is to pour only a very small amount in those huge glasses—much easier to hold.

TOASTING

While you have your glass in your hand, you may think of a toast that you wish to make, but it may not be your turn. Traditionally, the host makes the first toast. The remainder of the party may now chime in.

If toasted, do not stand during the toast. You may stand after the toast and then give your own.

BRINGING A BOTTLE TO THE RESTAURANT

If you wish to take a bottle, make sure the restaurant does not carry that specific wine; it would not be polite to bring a bottle the restaurant offers.

You could check the menu first so that you could pair the wine with the food.

Taking more than one wine is not very polite. Besides the corkage fee, it appears as if you are moving in.

If you take a particularly fine wine, offer a taste to the wine steward or sommelier. This is always a very polite gesture and is appreciated.

TAKING UNFINISHED WINE HOME

On taking an unfinished bottle of wine home, please do so. It is appropriate and it makes sense.

If the restaurant does not allow it, perhaps this is an indication that this place is not for you. California's State Business and Professions Code states that restaurants can allow any guest to remove a partially consumed bottle of wine from the premises upon their departure. It is that "*can*" that could be a problem. Check with your state's position on this as well.

ENTERTAINING

Hosting a dinner or special occasion event for friends and family is exciting. Designing a menu and choosing just the right wine to pair with each course is part of that excitement. A simple rule may help with the pairing.

Match heavy-to-heavy and light-to-light, which is called mirroring. For example, pair a dish with cream with a Chardonnay, because both are heavy.

Alternatively, contrasting the wine with the food may be your best choice, such as a nice Sauvignon Blanc with macaroni and cheese. The wine is light and crisp, while the food is heavy.

We no longer believe that the only wine served with chicken must be white. For example, the chicken could be in a heavy marinara. A Chianti or Zinfandel would be a nice option in this case. Thus, consider the spices, herbs, and sauces.

A Pinot Noir or Sauvignon Blanc usually pair well with most foods. In addition, always choose the wine you like to drink.

GREAT SOURCES

- "Wine Spectator's" shopping list
- Food and Wine
- Wine Spectator
- Food and Wine Pairing.org

Start the evening with lighter wines or sparkling wine. It is best to drink light to dark or heavy. For example, pour a Champagne first and then a Merlot. This is much the same as your choice in food. You would have the appetizers before the roast beef or the Brie before the heavily spiced chicken.

WHAT TO DO WITH THE GIFT BOTTLE

If a guest brings a bottle of wine, should you open it? It really is your choice, but at the very least, it is polite to ask the guest if they would like it to be opened.

The guest may mention that the wine is for your collection, if so, thank the generous person, put the wine away and ask them back soon. I usually mention that I should share this wonderful wine so that I may learn the wishes of the guest.

PROVIDE NON-ALCOHOL ALTERNATIVES

To ensure the safe drive home and to satisfy those who do not drink, provide plenty of water and other non-alcoholic beverages. Alcohol is dehydrating so offer water often. For those who do drink, plan on having approximately ¾ to one bottle of wine per person.

WHAT IF YOU ARE THE GUEST?

Take a bottle of wine that you enjoy or perhaps a wine that you've wanted to try. Better yet, if the host is a close friend, you may wish to take a cherished bottle from your collection. As in all things, consider the receiver of the wine.

If your friend is a Chardonnay lover, take Chardonnay. It does not have to be an expensive bottle. My best friend loves a certain type of Chardonnay, so I always take at least one bottle when visiting him.

Most importantly, while sharing the wine, make a toast to Bacchus, the god of wine, for allowing mere humans to indulge in this gift from the heavens.

FREQUENTLY ASKED QUESTIONS

Why is the Pinot Noir and Chardonnay bottle the same shape, while the Cabernet is another?

The bottle shapes are traditional French styles. Pinot Noirs are traditionally Burgundian wines, as are Chardonnays, while Cabernets are a Bordeaux wine.

Do I spit when I taste at a winery?

It is your choice. Not many Californians are comfortable spitting in public, which is unfortunate. Spitting would allow the taster to sample more wines and not feel the effects of the alcohol as much.

Which wine do I taste first?

Always taste dry before sweet, light before heavy, young before old, and usually white before red.

When wine tasting in a winery, what do I do with the bottles I purchase?

Please remember to take an ice chest with plenty of ice to store your purchases until you get home.

Do I rinse my glass before switching wines?

No, wine and water do not mix well. A small amount of wine will not affect the taste of another.

Why are some bottles green?

Green bottles protect the wine from sunlight, which can heat and destroy the wine.

What about the shapes of bottles?

As stated above, the shapes are traditionally French. The shape represents the region the wines originate from, or as it is here, the varietal.

Where should I store my wines?

Store your prizes in a cool, slightly humid, dark place. The bottles should be stored horizontally.

What glass is best for wine tasting?

A clear, clean, dry, tulip shaped glass. Ideally, it should be 200-230ml in size to facilitate swirling. The stem should be long enough to hold without touching the bowl of the glass.

YOUR AUTHOR

Your author, Rebecca Black, also known as The Polite One, recently retired from her company **Etiquette Now!** after a successful and rewarding 20+ years. As the owner and facilitator of her company, this retired elementary school teacher designed and presented custom etiquette workshops for the individual, corporate, governmental and educational client. Due to her extensive knowledge of the subject, she is also a well-respected author of etiquette books and lesson plans.

Considered an expert in the field, Rebecca answers etiquette questions (Q & A) and offers advice through her blogs: Got Etiquette Advice, Got Wedding Etiquette, and The Polite One's Insights.

Although for many years, Rebecca, focused her writing on etiquette issues, she is currently following her passion of writing fiction. A few of her most recent children's books also focus on the environment: *Save the Jellywonkers: Help Keep The Oceans Clean; Beware the Blackness, A Jellywonker Adventure;* and *The Tale of a Bear & Pony: A Yellowstone Adventure*

Please visit rebeccablackauthor.blogspot.com for more information about Rebecca's current news.

Connect with Us

https://www.facebook.com/ThePoliteOne

https://www.facebook.com/rebeccablackauthor/

Visit Us

Rebecca Black Author

Etiquette Now! Insights

Got Etiquette Advice

Got Wedding Etiquette

Living Well & Enjoying Life—Rebecca Style

The Polite One's Insights

The Polite Traveler

https://www.amazon.com/author/rebecca_black

Published Fiction Books by Rebecca Black

The Tale of a Bear & Pony; A Yellowstone Adventure

Save The Jellywonkers! -- Help Keep Our Oceans Clean

Beware the Blackness! A Jellywonker Adventure

Sapphire and the Atlantians

War in Atlantis

The Return of the Tui Suri

Published Etiquette Books by Rebecca Black

Dining Etiquette: Essential Guide for Table Manners, Business Meals, Sushi, Wine and Tea Etiquette

Dress for All Occasions—The Basics, Attire Must-Haves, Dress Code Definitions & FAQs

Entertaining Skills 101

Etiquette for the Important Events in Our Lives: Common sense etiquette with a side of history and a dollop of gift-giving savvy

Etiquette for the Socially Savvy Adult: Life Skills for All Situations

Etiquette for the Socially Savvy Teen: Life Skills for All Situations

Golf Etiquette: Civility on the Course

How to Tea: British Tea Times

How to Teach Your Children Manners: Essential Life Skills Your Child Needs to Know!

International Business Travel Etiquette: Seal the Deal by Understanding Proper Protocol

Reaching Your Potential: How to use our life lessons to grow as a person and to improve the workplace environment

Societal Rage: Problem solving for our increasingly violent world

Sushi Etiquette: The guide for those who wish to eat sushi properly and avoid insulting the chef

Train the Trainer Guide: The essential guide for those who wish to present workshops and classes for adults

Wedding & Reception Planning: The Etiquette Guide for Planning the Perfect Wedding

Wine Etiquette--From holding the glass to ordering a bottle of wine in a restaurant and everything in-between

Workplace Etiquette: How to Create a Civil Workplace

Published Lesson Plans

Business Meal Etiquette

Career Fair Etiquette

Entertaining Skills 101: Lesson Plans for Those Who Wish to Present Workshops

Etiquette for the Socially Savvy Teen

Golf Etiquette

Growing Up Socially Savvy

How to Become a Socially Savvy Lady

How to Tea; British Tea Times

How to Teach Your Children Manners

Just for Teens, Skills for the Socially Savvy

Manners for Children

Organizational Skills

Prom Etiquette

Proper Business Attire

Skills for the Socially Savvy and Well-Dressed Teen

Skills for the Socially Savvy and Well-Organized Teen

Table Manners

Train the Trainer

Wine Etiquette

Workplace Etiquette

Wedding Lesson Plans

Lessons for the Newly Engaged
Wedding Planning
Wedding Reception Planning

Please visit https://www.amazon.com/author/rebecca_black for information about collecting more etiquette books.

Made in the USA
Monee, IL
17 March 2022

93009136R00077